Presented To:

From:

Date:

# 40 Days
## to Discovering
### the Real You

## Destiny Image Books by Dr. Cindy Trimm

*40 Day Soul Fast*

*40 Days to Discovering the Real You*

## Upcoming Releases in the Soul Fast Series

*Reclaim Your Soul*

*Reclaim Your Health*

# 40 Days
## to Discovering
### the Real You

LEARNING TO LIVE AUTHENTICALLY

## Dr. Cindy Trimm

AN INTERACTIVE SELF-DISCOVERY JOURNAL

DESTINY IMAGE® PUBLISHERS, INC.
P.O. Box 310, Shippensburg, PA 17257-0310
*"Promoting Inspired Lives."*

This book and all other Destiny Image, Revival Press, MercyPlace, Fresh Bread, Destiny Image Fiction, and Treasure House books are available at Christian bookstores and distributors worldwide.

For a U.S. bookstore nearest you, call 1-800-722-6774.
For more information on foreign distributors, call 717-532-3040.
Reach us on the Internet: www.destinyimage.com.

ISBN 13 TP: 978-0-7684-4029-4
ISBN 13 Ebook: 978-0-7684-8848-7

For Worldwide Distribution, Printed in the U.S.A.
3 4 5 6 7 8 9 10 / 16 15 14 13

# Contents

# Introduction

It is my own firm belief that the strength of the soul grows in proportion as you subdue the flesh.—Mohandas Gandhi

*Is not this the kind of fasting I have chosen: to loose the chains of injustice and untie the cords of the yoke, to set the oppressed free and break every yoke?* (Isaiah 58:6 NIV)

Welcome to *40 Days to Discovering the Real You!* The volume you hold in your hand will accompany you on this eight-week journey. I am on a mission to reconnect you with the true essence of a healthy soul—to lead you to a place in God where your soul can be healed—to reacquaint you with your authentic self. The next 40 days of getting to know the real you are going to be the best 40 days of your life! More importantly, when you learn to live authentically, from a healed, whole soul, no leaks, no punctures, no wounds—free and clear from

13

artificial, socially modified, cultural toxins—you will not only change your life, you will be poised to change the world.

We have all heard the phrases, "She's a beautiful soul," "Bless your soul," or "He's a mean old soul." These phrases describe our perception of an individual's nature or character. We are all "soul-people," and I believe that strengthening people at the level of their souls—restoring the soul and establishing it as the core and essence of who they really are as self-directed people of value, intelligence, and greatness— will change the world. We must break the false perception that as individuals, what we do does not make a difference in the greater scheme of things. We are as a nation, as a people, nothing more than the sum of our parts. As the giant world-changer, a small man by the name of Mohandas Gandhi, once said, "A nation's culture resides in the hearts and in the soul of its people." We will only be as whole and healed as a country as we are as a people. Oscar Wilde, the famous Irish poet and novelist said, *"Ordinary riches can be stolen, real riches cannot. In your soul are infinitely precious things that cannot be taken from you."* To reiterate a soul-searching question posed by Jesus, "What does it really profit us if we gain the whole world and lose our souls—the essence of who we really are and what it means to be human?"

If you are here reading this today, I imagine you have asked yourself that same question. For those of you looking to reclaim your soul and recapture the essence of who you really are, you are in the right place. I created this 40-Day Guide to guide you step-by-step, day-by-day, into a more authentic life. I am so glad you have chosen to join me on this journey to greater mental, emotional, and spiritual health! If you are looking to transform your life, you need look no further! Let the journey begin!

# What Is a Soul Fast?

The purpose of this *40 Day Soul Fast* is to not only bring health and restoration to the souls of individuals, but also to provide a mechanism for all people to learn to live from the inside out—from their authentic, God-nature selves. This Soul Fast is not addressing the issue of what you are eating, but what's eating you. The goal of this 40-day journey is to guide you through the process of discarding useless toxic emotions—self-sabotaging thoughts and viruses of the mind—so that you can fully move into who God created you to be. You will be invited to examine all of your objectives and relationships, any hidden agendas or motives that have governed your subconscious, in order to thrust you onto a new path of achievement and abundance. This journey is about setting you free once and for all to maximize your greatest potential.

*The 40-Day Soul Fast* takes place over eight weeks. For simplicity's sake, I have taken these eight weeks and divided them evenly so that you can establish a regular routine Monday through Friday, allowing for weekends off so you can focus on family and worship or make up a missed day if necessary.

Put aside time for "me-moments." Give yourself adequate time to focus on nurturing your inner self. Part of the soul fast discipline is not allowing everyday distractions to deter you from cultivating the inner life of your soul. It will require disciplined focus, a heightened mindfulness, and keen sensitivity to the Spirit of God.

We will begin our 40-day journey by talking about capacity building. Week one of our eight-week venture focuses on "The Power of 40: Enlarging Your Capacity." This theme is more fully explored in *The 40 Day Soul Fast*, but for the purposes of this journal, it ties together the five characteristics you will find in week one. In week two, we will talk about "The Purpose of a Soul Fast: The Self-Leadership Challenge." In week three, we will discuss "The Nature of the Soul: The Essence of You." In week four, we address "The Properties of Thought: You Are What You Think." Week five brings us to "The Importance of Identity: Becoming a Master by Mastering Your Mind." In week six we look at "The Power of Words: Healing the Hole in Your Soul." In week seven, we begin wrapping up by dealing with "The Power of Doing: God's Chosen Fast." And in week eight, we conclude by "Sealing the Healing: The Cleansing Power of Love."

The focus of this journal is on developing the 40 characteristics of an authentic person. These characteristics tie in with *The 40 Day Soul Fast*, but you can also use this guide by itself as a tool for focused self-exploration. Each day, you will read a meditation about one of the 40 characteristics of an authentic person. Then you will be given several "Action Steps" to consider as you put these characteristics into practice. Use the space provided to write your responses, reflections, meditations, and anything else God places on your heart as you delve into these powerful characteristics of authenticity.

# THE SOUL OF THE MATTER

> Be your authentic self. Your authentic self is who you are when you have no fear of judgment or before the world starts pushing you around and telling you who you're supposed to be. Your fictional self is who you are when you have a social mask on to please everyone else. Give yourself permission to be your authentic self. —Dr. Phil McGraw

This *40 Day Soul Fast* is about finding rest and restoration for your soul. When all is well with the souls of humanity, all will be well in the world. When you have peace in your soul, you will bring that peace to bear on the world around you— you will become the change you are hoping to see.

Over the next eight weeks, you will learn and grow and be empowered like never before to maximize your personal potential and break through to greater success.

May we all feel the presence of God each and every day as we *"do our best to enter that rest"* (Heb. 4:11 NLT). And as we take up residence there, may we become more acquainted with our authentic selves and equipped to walk in the light of what we discover.

Let this journal be a tool you can use to clear the ground of every obstruction and build a life of obedience into full maturity—the fully complete you! Are you ready to begin the best 40 days of your life?

Let the soul journey begin!

> *Beloved, I pray that you may prosper in all things and be in health, just as your soul prospers* (3 John 1:2 NKJV).

You don't have a soul. You are a Soul.—C. S. Lewis

# Week One

## The Power of Forty: Enlarging Your Capacity

Capacity building by learning to live authentically is what *The 40 Day Soul Fast* is all about. Capacity building, in a way, is also about community building. It's about growing into *"the fullness of God"* as a community (see Eph. 3 and 4).

During week one of *The 40 Day Soul Fast*, we will focus on how to build capacity by *Transforming, Cleansing, Aligning, Preparing,* and *Loosing.* I mention these topics here because they provide the framework for each of the 40 characteristics of an authentic person. However within the pages of this journal, we will only be focusing on the individual characteristics themselves.

The first characteristic we will highlight is *Awareness,* which relates to the focus of Day One—*Transforming.* Becoming aware of your current position is the first step in any transformation.

*Cleansing* is crucial to the beginning of any transformation— removing the impurities is necessary to make way for future growth and change. The characteristic of *Godliness* is your standard for cleanliness.

The characteristic of *Truth* is essential to the process of *Aligning* because Truth is what you need to be aligned *with*. We look at truth on this day as we continue to focus on our goal of capacity building.

*Preparing* takes *Commitment*. Commitment is a vital characteristic to focus on, and you will need to prepare for the rest of this fast by committing yourself to seeing this process through to the end.

Once you have committed, you will need to learn to practice *Patience*. Patience will help you last long enough to see what God is *Loosing* in your life—the manifestation of His truly wonderful plans for you. Rest assured you'll need to have built your capacity to be ready for it!

# Awareness

*God's Spirit touches our spirits and confirms who we really are* (Romans 8:15).

Today, the first day of your journey to a more authentic life, begins with a focus on *awareness*. This is the first of 40 characteristics that define a person who is living authentically—for how can you be truly yourself if you're not aware of who you truly are?

For now, I want you to simply focus on being more self-aware. Without cultivating self-awareness, nothing else you do will move you toward living more authentically. It is the first step you must take in making the adjustments necessary to correct the course of your life.

If you are to grow as a person, you must be aware of what your thoughts are telling you about whom you are now and who you are capable of becoming. You must have an objective understanding of your own mindsets, habits, challenges, strengths, and weaknesses.

We shall not cease from exploration—and the end of all our exploring will be to arrive where we started and know the place for the first time. —T. S. Eliot

## ACTION STEPS

- Describe what you believe are some outstanding characteristics about yourself.

_____

_____

_____

- How have you capitalized on those and harnessed the inherent power of you?

_____

_____

_____

_____

- What more can you do to maximize your unique set of gifts and minimize your own peculiar shortcomings?

_____

_____

_____

_____

- Take a look at the 24 questions in Appendix A. Spend some time looking them over at the beginning of this 40-day journey. You don't have to answer them all right now; return to reflect on them occasionally throughout the Soul Fast process. Insights will come to you along the way. When these questions keep you awake at night and make you listless during the day, set aside time to pray and journal your thoughts until you find the answers.

- Listen carefully to what you hear God's Spirit saying—that still, small voice—and write down what you hear.

_____

_____

_____

_____

_____

_____

_____

_____

_____

*Therefore if any person is [ingrafted] in Christ (the Messiah) he is a new creation (a new creature altogether); the old [previous moral and spiritual condition] has passed away. Behold, the fresh and new has come* (2 Corinthians 5:17 AMP).

# Godliness

*We're being shown how to turn our backs on a godless, indulgent life, and how to take on a God-filled, God-honoring life. This new life is starting right now, and is whetting our appetites for the glorious day when our great God and Savior, Jesus Christ, appears. He offered Himself as a sacrifice to free us from a dark, rebellious life into this good, pure life, making us a people He can be proud of, energetic in goodness* (Titus 2:12-14).

As we move through day two of our 40-day soul fast, I want to talk to you about the second characteristic of an authentic person: *Godliness*. Godliness begins with the "God-likeness" of your thoughts—the thoughts that govern your mind. It begins by putting on the mind of Christ.

As Paul wrote the Corinthians, *"Examine your motives, test your heart!"* (1 Cor. 11:27). Make sure everything you say, do, think, and choose is lined up with who it is you truly want to be. Check your heart. Clean house by sweeping up any impure motives or stray intentions. Pay attention to how the things you harbor within your heart affect your words and behaviors—and equally important, how your words, habits, and behaviors affect the life of your soul.

I encourage you today to do a thorough study of the word *godliness* and meditate on all it implies. Then ask yourself where you are falling short of it. Eliminate those things that are not "adding to your faith" and supplement those key things Peter listed that will *"have your life on a firm footing"* (2 Pet. 1:10)!

> True godliness does not turn men out of the world, but enables them to live better in it and excites their endeavors to mend it. —William Penn

## ACTION STEPS

- Meditate on the following and journal what you believe the Bible is saying about you as a person: God created human beings in His own image—reflecting His own nature. He blessed them saying: "Prosper! Reproduce! Fill Earth! Take charge!" (See Genesis 1:26-28.)

_____

_____

_____

_____

_____

- Sometimes we are our own worst enemy.
  Are you sabotaging your own success by the
  thoughts you think? Are you allowing those
  thoughts to interfere with how God wants you
  to view yourself? Are you giving someone else
  permission to lay things on you that aren't
  yours to carry and don't further you toward
  your destiny?

  _____

  _____

  _____

  _____

  _____

  _____

- Are your past failures holding dominion over
  your future? Are relationships distracting you,
  or worse, suppressing your God-like nature for
  greatness, significance, and love?

  _____

  _____

  _____

  _____

  _____

  _____

  _____

- In what areas are you living "a godless, indulgent life" and how can you—starting right now—begin living a more "God-filled, God-honoring life?"

  _____

  _____

  _____

  _____

- What undermining habits do you want God to help you to give up? List them and commit them to prayer. From this day onward, expect God to empower you to live a godly life pleasing to Him.

  _____

  _____

  _____

*Think of your sufferings as a weaning from that old sinful habit of always expecting to get your own way. Then you'll be able to live out your days free to pursue what God wants instead of being tyrannized by what you want* (1 Peter 4:1).

The way to be truly happy is to be truly human, and the way to be truly human is to be truly godly. —J. J. Packer

# Truth

*You with open minds; truth-ready minds will see it at once. Prefer my life-disciplines over chasing after money, and God-knowledge over a lucrative career. For Wisdom is better than all the trappings of wealth; nothing you could wish for holds a candle to her* (Proverbs 8:9-11).

As we progress on our journey toward authenticity, we have talked about being more self-aware and about the importance of pursuing godliness. To help us do both more fully, we must be willing to take an honest look at our lives and be willing to seek the truth about who we are now versus who God calls us to be in Christ.

The concept of truth has always been at the center of great debates amongst theologians and scientists. The foundational key to living authentically *is* truth. When truth is absent from our lives, it is impossible for the soul to be truly free. It is, therefore, a spiritual imperative that you should not only be true to yourself, but should continuously strive to live in the full light of the truth and to be governed by the Spirit of Truth. As the psalmist wrote, *"What you're after is truth from the inside out. Enter me, then; conceive a new, true life"* (Ps. 51:6).

Truth demands honesty. Those daring to live authentically must, first and foremost, be honest with themselves and others. Always speak the truth. Exemplify truth. Uphold the truth. Stand on the truth. *Live the truth!*

> Leaders of the future will have the courage to align with principles and go against the grain of old assumptions or paradigms. It takes tremendous courage and stamina to say, "I'm going to align my personal value system, my lifestyle, my direction, and my habits with timeless principles." —Stephen Covey

## ACTION STEPS

- Sit quietly with the Spirit of Truth and allow Him to guide you into all truth about who God has created you to be. (See John 16:13.)

_____

_____

_____

_____

_____

_____

_____

- Invite the Holy Spirit to reveal "deep and hidden things" about yourself that you should either embrace or change. (See Daniel 2:22.)

_____

_____

_____

_____

- Ask Him to help you filter through what is not of the truth, to cut anything away from your heart or mind that is not true, and to help you cultivate those things that lead *"to finding yourself, your true self"* (Luke 9:23).

_____

_____

_____

_____

- What would this new, true life look like if it were conceived in you?

_____

_____

_____

- How can you realign your life so that it reflects the authentic you God had in mind?

_____

_____

_____

_____

_____

_____

_____

_____

_____

*When the Spirit of truth comes, He will guide you into all truth. He will not speak on His own but will tell you what He has heard.* (John 16:13 NLT).

The truth is incontrovertible. Malice may attack it, ignorance may deride it, but in the end, there it is.
—Winston Churchill

# Commitment

*Self-sacrifice is the way, My way, to saving yourself, your true self. What good would it do to get everything you want and lose you, the real you? What could you ever trade your soul for?* (Mark 8:37)

The difference between those who win at life and those who lose is not based on the amount of education one acquires, the amount of money one earns, nor the superior skills one was born with, but instead is based upon one's level of commitment. Commitment requires faith. You must not only have faith in God, but faith in the person that God has made you to be. That faith will be tested along the way.

The testing and trying of your faith, the refining of your intentions and resolve, the dedication, determination, and perseverance required to stick with something until you've obtained the desired outcome will empower and liberate you—and expand your capacity to do even more. Jesus told

His disciples, *"By your steadfastness and patient endurance you shall win the true life of your souls"* (Luke 21:19 AMP).

If you are reading this, you have already demonstrated this characteristic and are well on your way to living truer to your authentic self. Continue to cultivate commitment by sticking with this 40-day endeavor to the very end! It is this steadfast endurance that will strengthen and purify your soul like nothing else.

> A little more persistence, a little more effort, and what seemed hopeless failure may turn to glorious success. —Elbert Hubbard

## ACTION STEPS

- In light of "thinking bigger," what would your life look like if you were to actually "win the true life of your soul?" Imagine it now.

_____

_____

_____

_____

- What are you going to commit to doing in order to save the real you?

_____

_____

_____

_____

- Identify one thing you should purge from your life that is causing you to lose the real you.

_____

_____

_____

_____

_____

_____

- Now identify one thing you could add that will help cultivate your truest self.

_____

_____

_____

_____

_____

_____

_____

*Staying with it—that's what is required. Stay with it to the end. You won't be sorry* (Luke 21:19).

# Patience

*We continue to shout our praise even when we're hemmed in with troubles, because we know how troubles can develop passionate patience in us, and how that patience in turn forges the tempered steel of virtue, keeping us alert for whatever God will do next* (Romans 5:3).

Yesterday we talked about commitment. Once you've committed to an endeavor, you will need patience to see it through to completion.

Patience will refine and perfect you. Patience is a discipline you must practice if you want to break free from the myriad of things that can plague and pollute your soul!

Jesus said that it is only by exercising patience that you will learn to *"possess your soul"* (Luke 21:19). As you draw closer to your authentic self, you must learn to take possession of your soul by mastering the art of patience.

Developing patience is key to growing into your authentic self and fulfilling your best destiny: *"For you have need of steadfast patience and endurance, so that you may perform and fully accomplish the will of God"* (Heb. 10:36 AMP).

If one advances confidently in the direction of his dreams and endeavors to live the life which he has imagined, he will meet with a success unexpected in common hours. —Henry David Thoreau

## ACTION STEPS

- What typically causes you to lose your patience?

_____

_____

_____

_____

- How can you change your perspective to tap into the power of patience?

_____

_____

_____

_____

- Visualize yourself exercising patient restraint the next time you want to react otherwise.

_____

_____

_____

_____

*Let patience have its perfect work, that you may be perfect and complete, lacking nothing* (James 1:4 NKJV).

# Week Two

# The Purpose of a Soul Fast: The Self-Leadership Challenge

Fasting is about restraining your natural pleasures and breaking the cycle of stressful living by taking the time to seek God's face, the only One who sees your heart and knows who the authentic you really is. God has the power to break through the clutter that masks your identity, distracts your focus, and keeps you from the abundant life that Jesus died to provide. Your focus areas in developing the self-leadership to accomplish this soul fast are *Connecting, Healing, Empowering, Directing,* and *Seeing.*

The purpose of fasting is to re-connect with God, allowing Him to set you free of those things that weigh you down. *Connecting* with God increases your *Capacity!*

Fasting allows the Holy Spirit to reshape you into your true self by dealing with your wounds from the past that have distorted, stagnated, and stunted your essence. As you work through your *Healing,* you are moving toward the characteristic of *Wholeness.*

41

As you seek God's *Empowering* in order to reach your full capacity, it is very important to focus on *Balance*. This keeps you from seeking power for selfish purposes and allows you to dedicate the gifts of God back to His service.

During this soul fast, you will discover an increased ability to discern and follow God's direction. The more you are able to practice *Directing* to bring your ways into alignment with His, the more *Peace* you will have in your life.

Practicing the skill of *Seeing* will allow you to discover the possibilities God wants to show you in unexpected places. What will you see? His *Goodness* becoming real to you.

# Capacity

*The unspiritual self, just as it is by nature, can't receive the gifts of God's Spirit. There's no capacity for them* (1 Corinthians 2:14).

All human beings are born with capacity. Among the many things we have capacity for is the capacity to grow, to learn, to love, to create, to change, to modify our behavior based on the demands of the situation or circumstance, to succeed, and to prosper. The purpose of The 40 Day Soul Fast is to create in you the capacity to hear and receive God's best plan for your life – to enlarge the capacity of your soul for the great work that lies ahead of us all. May you be among those, as Jesus said, *"to whom* [the capacity to receive] *it has been given"* (Matt. 19:11 AMP).

Take time to reflect on what you are hearing the Lord say this week. Press in and focus on discerning the Lord's voice amidst all the static and clutter around you. Clear the ground wherever you are by making room for the presence of

God—let Him come and burn up the overgrowth and chaff in your life.

Every day of this 40-day soul fast you should be growing more spiritually alive! You should be increasing your capacity to access everything God's Spirit is doing!

> Where the spirit does not work with the hand there is no art. —Leonardo da Vinci

## ACTION STEPS

- What have you learned about yourself so far?

_____

_____

_____

_____

_____

- What are four things you will purpose to eliminate?

_____

_____

_____

_____

_____

- What four new habits will you focus on cultivating?

_____

_____

_____

_____

*Make the most of what God gives, both the bounty and the capacity to enjoy it, accepting what's given and delighting in the work* (Ecclesiastes 5:19).

# Wholeness

*Instead of worrying, pray. Let petitions and praises shape your worries into prayers, letting God know your concerns. Before you know it, a sense of God's wholeness, everything coming together for good, will come and settle you down. It's wonderful what happens when Christ displaces worry at the center of your life* (Philippians 4:6).

When I pause to consider the course of my life, I conclude that it was divinely orchestrated to bring me to a place of wholeness. Denying, rejecting, judging, or hiding from any aspect of your total being creates pain and results in a lack of wholeness. You cannot adjust what you are not prepared to address.

You are the sum total of all your experiences—good and bad. Wholeness represents a total integration of every

47

facet of your life's experiences. It is the only way to live with congruency, interconnectedness, and completeness.

You can only be complete if your heart is not divided between blame and acceptance. Wholeness requires you to accept responsibility for what you choose to let inhabit your heart.

The one quality that authentic people have is their willingness to take responsibility for their life. When you allow faith and forgiveness to liberate and heal your soul, you will be well on your way to living on the summit of wholeness.

Allow God's Spirit to bring healing to your heart, wholeness to your soul, and that degree of completion we all long for. Paul told the Colossians, *"You are complete in Him"* (Col. 2:10).

> Nothing can cure the soul but the senses, just as nothing can cure the senses but the soul. —Oscar Wilde

## ACTION STEPS

- Identify your most pressing concerns. What causes you to lie awake at night and worry? What distracts you and causes you to furrow your brow throughout the day? Who or what have you allowed to steal your peace?

_____

_____

_____

- Make a commitment to yourself to never wish things did not happen. Accept, learn, and grow from every experience.

_____

_____

_____

_____

- Take responsibility by shaping every irritation, offense, anxiety, or doubt into a prayer. Write down what you notice happens as a result. Who are you able to forgive? How will this affect your network of relationships?

_____

_____

_____

_____

*May God Himself, the God who makes everything holy and whole, make you holy and whole, put you together—spirit, soul, and body—and keep you fit for the coming of our Master, Jesus Christ* (1 Thessalonians 5:23).

# Balance

*For he who has once entered [God's] rest also has
ceased from [the weariness and pain] of human
labors* (Hebrews 4:10 AMP).

One of the primary reasons for pursuing a soul fast is to
regain balance in life. What is life balance? It can be hard
to describe exactly. A balanced life will look different to
different people. But I'm sure we would all agree what it feels
like when your life is out of balance! I believe that is why many
of you are on this soul fast journey. You are seeking balance.

A balanced life is about prioritizing the many activities
and responsibilities involved in living—work, home, health,
parenting, finances, marriage, etc.—and framing them in
such a way that you do not lose touch with yourself in the
process. And then, when life throws you a curve ball, you are
still able to hit a homerun.

Creating balance requires taking a deep breath and
finding time in an otherwise busy schedule to nurture yourself

and others. Balance is not only about prioritizing what you do, but is also about getting adequate rest. As with wholeness, this comes when you put your entire life into God's hands and allow Him to lead. When your priorities are right, you will feel less stressed and more blessed.

Gaining balance for me began by seeking the Kingdom of God and making His will a priority (see Matt. 6:33). If whatever you do is done "as unto the Lord"—with a grateful heart—not seeking anything but to please God, you will find your life naturally lining up with God's perfect will and infused by His perfect peace

If you are first and foremost honoring God with your every thought and deed, then His peace, joy, and rest will always be near at hand. Remember, this is God's will concerning you!

Opening your whole being to be an instrument and voice from God, takes something from you as you allow God to work through you, pouring yourself out; empowerment from the Spirit is a rhythm of work and rest. —Marlaena Cochran

## ACTION STEPS

This week, I encourage you to read Hebrews 4:1-11.

- How does it feel to rest in God?

_____

_____

_____

_____

- What do you need to change in your daily routine to bring true balance?

_____

_____

_____

_____

_____

*Bless the Lord, oh my soul, and forget not all His benefits: who forgives all your iniquities, who heals all your diseases, who redeems your life from destruction, who crowns you with loving kindness and tender mercies, who satisfies your mouth with good things, so that your youth is renewed like the eagle's* (Psalms 103:2-5 NKJV).

# Peace

*Whoever wants to embrace life and see the day fill up with good, here's what you do: Say nothing evil or hurtful; snub evil and cultivate good; run after peace for all you're worth. God looks on all this with approval...but He turns His back on those who do evil things* (1 Peter 3:10-12).

If a state of peace is essential for health and prosperity to flourish in a nation, how much more in our individual lives? For this reason Paul told Timothy to pray for *"all who are in authority so that we can live peaceful and quiet lives marked by godliness and dignity"* (1 Tim. 2:2 NLT).

This week practice peace: *"Let the peace of Christ rule in your hearts, since as members of one body you were called to peace"* (Col. 3:15 NIV). How do you practice peace? How do you let the peace of Christ rule in your heart? I leave you with these instructions given by the apostle Peter:

*Summing up: Be agreeable, be sympathetic, be loving, be compassionate, be humble. That goes for all of you, no exceptions. No retaliation. No sharp-tongued sarcasm. Instead, bless—that's your job, to bless. You'll be a blessing and also get a blessing* (1 Peter 3:8-9).

If there is light in the soul, there will be beauty in the person. If there is beauty in the person, there will be harmony in the house. If there is harmony in the house, there will be order in the nation. If there is order in the nation, there will be peace in the world.
—Chinese Proverb

## ACTION STEPS

- Mohandas Gandhi said, "Each one of us has to find his peace from within. And peace to be real must be unaffected by outside circumstances." Jesus said, "Let not your heart be troubled." Think of some practical things you can do in your life today to manifest peace.

_____

_____

_____

_____

_____

_____

_____

- Focus on allowing the peace of Christ to rule in your heart. When Christ's peace rules your inner world, how will that affect your outer world?

_____

_____

_____

_____

- Be willing to let go of whatever does not produce peace. Pray, and write down anything the Spirit brings to your mind.

_____

_____

_____

_____

*This core holy people will not do wrong. They won't lie, won't use words to flatter or seduce. Content with who they are and where they are, unanxious, they'll live at peace* (Zephaniah 3:12-13).

# Goodness

*Each person has inside a basic decency and goodness. If he listens to it and acts on it, he is giving a great deal of what it is the world needs most. It is not complicated but it takes courage. It takes courage for a person to listen to his own goodness and act on it. —Pablo Casals*

Paul posed one of the most compelling questions when he challenged the Romans:

*You surely don't think much of God's wonderful goodness or of His patience and willingness to put up with you. Don't you know that the reason God is good to you is because He wants you to turn to Him?* (Romans 2:4 CEV)

It is the goodness of God that leads to repentance. It is only because of God's goodness that we can have any hope of being good ourselves.

One of the most detoxifying things you can do for your soul is to turn to God and repent. When you turn away from thoughts and habits that are contrary to the Spirit of Christ, and instead turn toward God and His ways, you become "rich in goodness." As Paul told the Romans: *"You yourselves are rich in goodness, amply filled with all [spiritual] knowledge"* (Rom. 15:14 AMP).

Get re-acquainted with your authentic self. Determine to be filled with God's goodness, and to express it.

> After the knowledge of, and obedience to, the will of God, the next aim must be to know something of His attributes of wisdom, power, and goodness as evidenced by His handiwork. —James Prescott Joule

## ACTION STEPS

- Examine your life, your habits, your heart, and your thoughts: Are they an expression of the life of Christ in you, "rich in goodness"?

---

---

---

---

---

---

- How might these things be different if they consisted of "every form of goodness"?

_____

_____

_____

_____

_____

- Think of one negative thing you can replace with something positive.

_____

_____

_____

_____

_____

*For the fruit...of the Light or the Spirit [consists] in every form of kindly goodness, uprightness of heart, and trueness of life* (Eph. 5:9 AMP).

# Week Three

## The Nature of the Soul: The Essence of You

The soul is that aspect of your whole being that correlates, integrates, and enlivens everything going on in the various dimensions of your self—things like your appetites, ambitions, thoughts, and motivations. It's what makes you, you.

Disaster happens when your soul becomes organized around feelings. A negative feeling or prevailing mood can spread into your whole life; like a red towel in a load of white clothes—it bleeds on everything.

However, God also gave you emotions that would incline you to enjoy participating in life—as well as to turn you away from desires that could keep you in bondage and morph into full-blown lusts.

The key isn't to deny or repress your feelings—but to control them. As you explore the nature of the soul this week, your characteristics of authenticity are connected to the themes of *Becoming, Restoring, Resting, Imaging,* and *Sensing.*

The soul isn't something you have, but rather who you are. *Becoming* your authentic self—your true soul—will take a considerable amount of this day's characteristic—*Discipline*.

The key to *Restoring* your soul is living what you believe in every dimension of your life. This is possible when your life is defined by the characteristic of *Simplicity*.

Resting allows your soul to recharge and connect back to God. The characteristic linked to *Resting* is *Uniqueness*. Take time to rest and thank God for making you uniquely *you*.

*Imaging* means representing God on this earth—showing the world His image in you—and one of the most powerful ways you can do this is through your unique, God-given *Passion*.

Everyone has feelings and relates to the world largely through *Sensing*—their ability to feel. However, the soul should never be controlled by emotions. Instead, learn to embrace God's *Joy*, which should define your authentic life. When you are characterized by joy, you're living out of who you really are!

Day
Eleven

# Discipline

*Exercise daily in God—no spiritual flabbiness,
please! Workouts in the gymnasium are
useful, but a disciplined life in God is far
more so, making you fit both today and forever*
(1 Timothy 4:6).

The key to a successful, prosperous life is discipline. Paul emphasized the importance of discipline in almost every letter he wrote. In the Book of Acts he said, *"I always exercise and discipline myself...to have a clear (unshaken, blameless) conscience, void of offense toward God and toward men"* (Acts 24:16 AMP).

Paul wrote Timothy declaring: *"God has not given us a spirit of fear and timidity, but of power, love, and self-discipline"* (2 Tim. 1:7 NLT).

Peter also wrote about discipline: *"So don't lose a minute in building on what you've been given, complementing your basic faith with...alert discipline"* (2 Pet. 1:5).

A disciplined life in God will produce the fruit of the Spirit: *"love, joy, peace, patience, kindness, goodness, faithfulness, gentleness, and self-control"* (Gal. 5:22-23 NLT). Discipline will empower you to become and to do the extraordinary.

> Moral excellence comes about as a result of habit. We become just by doing just acts, temperate by doing temperate acts, brave by doing brave acts. —Aristotle

## ACTION STEPS

- How do we exercise a disciplined life in God?

_____

_____

_____

_____

- Paul said the discipline of God is not so much about what we choose *not* to do, but more about what we choose *to* do. Make a list of things you can actively choose to do for God.

_____

_____

_____

_____

_____

_____

- Discipline starts in the mind. For every negative thought or negative word you think or speak today, commit to give $1.00 to a charity of your choice.

_____

_____

_____

_____

*Get out there and walk—better yet, run—on the road God called you to travel. ...Do this with humility and discipline—not in fits and starts, but steadily, pouring yourselves out for each other in acts of love* (Ephesians 4:1-3).

# Simplicity

*Here's what I want you to do: Find a quiet, secluded place so you won't be tempted to role-play before God. Just be there as simply and honestly as you can manage. The focus will shift from you to God, and you will begin to sense His grace* (Matthew 6:5-6).

The 40 days of Lent, as with any fast, represents a period of time set aside for keeping the main thing the main thing—for focusing on what is important in our lives as children of God. It's essential that we don't get distracted by "dos" and "don'ts," but remain focused on the power of hoping and believing in Christ as evidenced by our love for one another.

Simplicity does not mean that things are simpler or less demanding. It means that anything superfluous and not needed is discarded and replaced by what is necessary. The Bible states over and over that it is not sacrifice but obedience the Lord seeks—and our love walk demonstrates that obedience. We know we are led of the Spirit when we choose love.

Keep it simple. Walk in love. This is how you will uncover your authentic self, created in the image of love. Just be yourself before God, for God loves you just as you are! And being yourself before Him is how you can love Him in return. Love being yourself.

> True religion is real living; living with all one's soul, with all one's goodness and righteousness. —Albert Einstein

## ACTION STEPS

- How does the geography of your soul look? Do you need to establish order, repair the power lines, or just mend some fences? Make a list of what these are and begin to address them immediately.

_____

_____

_____

_____

_____

_____

_____

_____

- Today, feed your soul by pursuing the simplicity demonstrated by Christ—demonstrate love. List some practical things you can do to show this.

_____

_____

_____

_____

_____

_____

*You have purified your souls in obeying the truth through the Spirit in sincere love of the brethren, love one another fervently with a pure heart* (1 Peter 1:22 NKJV).

Day
Thirteen

# Uniqueness

*You shaped me first inside, then out; You formed
me in my mother's womb...body and soul, I am
marvelously made! What a creation! You know
me inside and out, You know every bone in my
body; You know exactly how I was made, bit-
by-bit, how I was sculpted from nothing into
something. Like an open book, You watched me
grow...the days of my life all prepared before I'd
even lived one day* (Psalm 139:14).

Your soul is what makes you uniquely you. Your soul is
imprinted with an eternally unique DNA that holds within
it the keys to your purpose, potential, and destiny. I say
"eternally unique" because nobody in the history of the world
has ever been—or ever will be—just like you.

Today, I want you to stir up the unique expression of
God's glory and grace He has woven into your soul—the
divine essence of your being. Call out and celebrate those

things that make you uniquely you. Be grateful for the gift God created you to be! Rejoice in the wonder and majesty that is you!

> To have a firm persuasion in our work—to feel that what we do is right for ourselves and good for the world at the same exact time—is one of the great triumphs of human existence. —David Whyte

## ACTION STEPS

Meditate on the following:

> Each second we live is a new and unique moment of the universe, a moment that will never be again. And what do we teach our children? We teach them that two and two make four and that Paris is the capital of France. When will we also teach them what they are? We should say to each of them: Do you know what you are? You are a marvel. You are unique. In all the years that have passed, there has never been another child like you. Your legs, your arms, your clever fingers; the way you move. You may become a Shakespeare, a Michelangelo, or a Beethoven. You have the capacity for anything. —Pablo Picasso

> If a man does not keep pace with his companions, perhaps it is because he hears a different drummer. Let him step to the music which he hears, however measured or far away. —Henry David Thoreau

- List five aspects of your personality that make you special.

_____

_____

_____

- List five desires that are uniquely yours.

_____

_____

_____

- List five strengths that you bring to the table.

_____

_____

_____

- List five talents that God has given you to steward.

_____

_____

_____

*I will praise You, for I am fearfully and wonderfully made; marvelous are Your works, and that my soul knows very well* (Psalm 139:14).

# Passion

*God's holy people passionately and faithfully
stand their ground* (Revelation 13:10).

Yesterday we talked about the importance of embracing your uniqueness. Today I want to talk to you about the importance of embracing your passions. It is passion that gives us eyes to see what is possible, and the fortitude to pursue it. Passion will cause you to take risks and stand against the odds: *"God's holy people passionately and faithfully stand their ground"* (Rev. 13:9).

The things you are passionate about are God-given desires. God's desires in you will move you out of the egocentric, self-centered realm you would otherwise occupy. They cause you to live on a higher plane and tap into the dimension of supernatural ability and resources.

When work, commitment, and pleasure all become one and you reach that deep well where passion lives, nothing is impossible. —Nancy Coey

## ACTION STEPS

- What are you passionate about?

_____

_____

_____

_____

_____

_____

_____

- How can you harness the power of your passions to establish yourself, take dominion, and make a difference within your family, community, or country?

_____

_____

_____

_____

_____

_____

_____

- Your inherent passions are part of your genetic makeup. How can you tap into your passions to "go and do your best?"

_____

_____

_____

_____

_____

_____

*You do so well in so many things—you trust God, you're articulate, you're insightful, you're passionate, you love— now go and do your best* (2 Corinthians 8:5).

# Joy

*May the God of hope fill you with all joy and peace in believing, that you may abound in hope by the power of the Holy Spirit* (Romans 15:13 NKJV).

The characteristic of joy—and joyfulness—is one of the most, if not *the* most, significant and telling traits of an authentic person. It demonstrates, as well as determines, successful authentic living in so many ways.

Jesus came to empower you to maximize your joy because joy is your key to victory and a more vibrant and satisfying life. Joy is not only healing and restorative, but it is a powerful spiritual force. Jesus sought to teach you how to harness the raw power of simple joy. As the author and finisher of our faith, Jesus tapped into the power of joy to enable Him to endure the Cross (see Heb. 12:2). Now that's powerful.

If the sight of the blue skies fills you with joy, if a blade of grass springing up in the fields has power to move you, if the simple things in nature have a message you understand, rejoice, for your soul is alive. —Eleanora Duse

## ACTION STEPS

- How can you stir up joy in your everyday life? Be specific.

_____

_____

_____

_____

- Discouragement, loss, depression, disappoint-ment, fear, anxiety, oppression, sickness, lack, and loneliness are common joy-thieves. What are some of the things stealing your joy? What will you do to eliminate them?

_____

_____

_____

_____

_____

_____

*The joy of the Lord is your strength and stronghold* (Nehemiah 8:10 AMP).

# Week Four

## The Properties of Thought: You Are What You Think

There is scientifically measurable power to your thoughts. Your thoughts are all of the ways you are conscious of reality—they form your reality—your memories, beliefs, ideas, and images. Most of these ways of knowing reside so deeply in you that it is hard to tell which may be affecting your life. You will never have more, or go farther, or accomplish greater things than your thoughts will allow. But as quickly as light illuminates a room, a single thought can shed new light on your life, changing everything including your destiny. Changing your thinking is about *Believing, Receiving, Focusing, Envisioning,* and *Conquering.*

One of the most compelling reasons for journeying toward authenticity is to uncover the genuine beauty of your truest self. *Believing* in that *Beauty* makes it a fact in your mind, and your thoughts determine your reality.

Receiving messages from God can happen when you embrace the characteristic of *Effortlessness*—not striving, conniving, manipulating, or clamoring to get ahead, but just *being* and letting God speak to you.

*Focusing* your mind is like setting the sails on a sailboat. Bring all your thinking to one focus—*Authenticity*. Living out of your truest self—who God created you to be.

The ability to harness your imagination to picture the possibilities before you is called *Envisioning*. It will take a lot of *Focus* to keep that vision foremost in your mind.

As we conclude our focus on our thought life, remember that you have an enemy out there, and he is attacking your thoughts. Set yourself on *Conquering* the enemy's tactics. To do this you must exhibit the characteristic of *Order*. An ordered life allows you to keep your focus set, in spite of the attacks that try to sway you, and keep your thought life determined by authenticity.

# Beauty

*If God gives such attention to the appearance of wildflowers—most of which are never even seen—don't you think He'll attend to you, take pride in you, do His best for you?"* (Matthew 6:30)

One of the most compelling reasons for journeying toward authenticity is to uncover the genuine beauty of your truest self. It is a process of peeling away the layers of artificial roles we so often play and the lies and limitations we impose on our own souls.

True beauty comes from within—which lends truth to the statement: "Beauty is as beauty does." Beauty is also in the eye of the beholder. Mohandas Gandhi said, "When I admire the wonders of a sunset or the beauty of the moon, my soul expands in the worship of the creator."

The beauty you see is a result of the beauty emanating from your own soul. Though many say that life is not a bed of roses, I believe that it is. Like a rose, if you judge it by the prick of its thorns and cast it aside as painful, you will miss its beauty. Sometimes people miss beauty because it is uncomfortable or unfamiliar. Try to find the beauty in things and people beyond the obvious.

When I think of cultivating "beauty of soul," I think of a soul's originality, vibrancy, and richness—awe-provoking intricacy and complexity of color—great depths and heights of potential—and the human soul's immense capacity to reflect God's glory.

Your soul is beautiful if for no other reason than it was created to express the divine magnificence of the Creator.

Insomuch as love grows in you, so in you beauty grows. For love is the beauty of the soul. —St. Augustine

## ACTION STEPS

- What would it look like to relax and "respond to God's giving"—to simply *be still and rest in the Lord; wait for Him and patiently lean yourself upon Him; fret not yourself*" (Ps. 37:7 AMP)? What kind of a beauty treatment would that be for your soul?

_____

_____

_____

_____

- Create space in your life for a spiritual beauty spa. Soak in God's presence. Allow God's Spirit to wash away any impurities, to peel away the old, dead things and soften the rough places.

_____

_____

_____

_____

_____

- Stop striving. Stop fussing. Relax in the beautiful you God created you to be and worship Him in that beauty.

*Worship the Lord in the beauty of holiness* (Psalm 96:9 NKJV).

# Effortlessness

*He energizes those who get tired...those who
wait upon God get fresh strength. They spread
their wings and soar like eagles, they run and
don't get tired; they walk and don't lag behind*
(Isaiah 40:28-29).

We don't often think of "effortlessness" as a characteristic
we should cultivate in our lives. Most of us were raised to always
try harder and do more in order to maximize our potential.
Although my life mission *is* to empower people to maximize
their potential, I believe the key is not in maximizing one's
*"doing"* as much as one's *"being."*

When I think of effortlessness, I think of entering God's
rest—a major theme throughout the Bible. Living authentically has much to do with living effortlessly—not striving,
conniving, manipulating, clamoring to get ahead, etc.

When you rest in God, you are operating from a place
of supernatural power, causing everything you do to seem

effortless. It may take effort to enter that place, but it will energize you once you're there.

> Repose is a quality too many undervalue. In the clamor one is irresistibly drawn to the woman who sits gracefully relaxed, who keeps her hands still, talks in a low voice, and listens with responsive eyes and smiles. She creates a spell around her, charming to the ear, the eye and the mind. —Good Housekeeping, November 1947

## ACTION STEPS

- Where do you need more "know how"—or where in your life are you feeling opposition or boxed in? What does *not* feel effortless?

_____

_____

_____

_____

- Try putting effort instead into pursuing God's rest. Practice "being still" and trusting God to lift you up so you soar—no, *vault*—effortlessly over the highest fences.

_____

_____

_____

_____

- Keep company with God so you learn to live freely and lightly.

_____

_____

_____

_____

*Walk with Me and work with Me—watch how I do it. Learn the unforced rhythms of grace. I won't lay anything heavy or ill-fitting on you. Keep company with Me and you'll learn to live freely and lightly* (Matthew 11:29-30).

# Authenticity

*Examine yourselves to see if your faith is genuine.*
*Test yourselves* (2 Corinthians 13:5 NLT).

This week we have been talking about the nature of the soul. Your soul is the divine, eternal essence of you. An uncluttered, healed, and whole soul represents your true, authentic self. Learning to living authentically is the purpose of this 40-day journey.

So what is authenticity?

Authenticity simply means being true to who you are—aligning your every thought and action with who and what you were created to be and do.

Judy Garland stated, "Always be a first-rate version of yourself instead of a second-rate version of someone else." Steve Jobs gave the following advice: "Your time is limited, so don't waste it living someone else's life. Don't be trapped by dogma, which is living with the results of other people's thinking. Don't let the noise of other's opinions drown out your own inner voice. And most importantly, have the courage to follow your heart and intuition. They somehow already know what you truly want to become. Everything else is secondary." While Charles Evans Hughes concluded, "When we lose the right to be different, we lose the privilege to be free."

Nothing or noone should define you—it is up to you to understand who you are and live according to that truth.

Take the lead in letting others step to the music they hear by dancing to your own.

That inner voice has both gentleness and clarity. So to get to authenticity, you really keep going down to the bone, to the honesty, and the inevitability of something. —Meredith Monk

## ACTION STEPS

- If God were to drop a plumb line into the building you've created of your life, how aligned would it be with His original blueprint for you? (See Amos 7:7-8.)

_____

_____

_____

_____

_____

_____

- How can you realign your life so that it reflects the authentic you God had in mind?

_____

_____

_____

_____

*What good would it do to get everything you want and lose you, the real you? What could you ever trade your soul for?* (Mark 8:34)

# Focus

*I've got my eye on the goal, where God is beckoning us onward...I'm off and running, and I'm not turning back...I focus on this one thing: forgetting the past and looking forward to what lies ahead...I keep focused on that goal. If any of you have something else in mind, something less than total commitment, God will clear your blurred vision—you'll see it yet! Now that we're on the right track, let's stay on it* (Philippians 3:12-15).

The number one thing that keeps people from realizing their goals, maximizing their potential, and fulfilling their purpose is focus. Wherever you place your focus - your mind, talents, abilities, and emotions will follow.

In other words, the life and reality you are experiencing are a reflection of the thoughts you are thinking. This is why you are told in Psalms to *"guard your heart above all else, for it determines the course of your life"* (Ps. 4:23 NLT). Ultimately, the power of our thoughts translates into our ability to focus. It's focused thought that wields the greatest power.

If you do not want to see something in your future, do not focus on it today. Train your mind to focus on the positive, and you will always have positive outcomes.

> Our thoughts create our reality—where we put our focus is the direction we tend to go. — Peter McWilliams

## ACTION STEPS

- What is God calling you to do? Focus on your calling, not your circumstances.

_____

_____

_____

_____

- What is it you want more of? If you want more of God and His power working in your life, focus on God and His power!

_____

_____

_____

_____

- Focus on what you want, not what you don't want! Do not allow anything or anyone to alter your focus.

_____

_____

_____

_____

*Keep your eyes straight ahead; ignore all sideshow distractions. Watch your step, and the road will stretch out smooth before you. Look neither right nor left; leave evil in the dust* (Proverbs 4:24-27).

# Order

*Look carefully then how you walk! Live purposefully and worthily and accurately, not as the unwise and witless, but as wise (sensible, intelligent people), Making the very most of the time [buying up each opportunity], because the days are evil. Therefore do not be vague and thoughtless and foolish, but understanding and firmly grasping what the will of the Lord is* (Ephesians 5:15-17 AMP).

Yesterday we talked about the power of focus. Sometimes it is a challenge to not only *set* our focus on what we should, but to *keep* our focus once we do. One of the tools—or characteristics—that will help you *stay* focused is learning to order your thoughts.

Nothing will help you keep order in your mind more than establishing order in your daily life. I'm talking about making the most of your time every day and eliminating "time wasters." If your day is cluttered or full of toxic activities, so will be your mind! Junk time is as bad as junk food! Take account of the empty time calories that make up the daily sustenance of your life in the form of television watching, Internet surfing, magazine perusing, or even gossiping with coworkers. As Paul told the Ephesians, *"Don't live carelessly, unthinkingly"* (Eph. 5:17)—*"make every minute count"* (Eph. 5:16 CEV).

This is the beginning of a new day. God has given me this day to use as I will. I can waste it or use it for good. What I do today is important, because I am exchanging a day of my life for it. When tomorrow comes, this day will be gone forever, leaving in its place something that I have traded for it. I want it to be gain, not loss; good not evil; success not failure; in order that I shall not regret the price I paid for it.
—Author Unknown

## ACTION STEPS

- As you sit quietly in the presence of God, take an account of how you spend or allocate each hour of each day, just like you keep an account of how you spend money or allocate calories.

_____

_____

_____

_____

_____

- How can you "reorder" your day to help you better order your thoughts?

_____

_____

_____

_____

_____

_____

- How does the order, or lack of order, in your home, office, car, or garage affect the order, or lack of order, in your soul? Is there room for more order? How will you bring that to pass? When?

_____

_____

_____

_____

_____

_____

_____

*Consider well the path of your feet, and let all your ways be established and ordered aright* (Proverbs 4:26 AMP).

# Week Five

## The Importance of Identity: Becoming a Master by Mastering Your Mind

Who are you really? Have you ever asked yourself that question in earnest? Most of us are so focused on what we do day-to-day—often struggling to meet the expectations of others—that we don't stop to ask who we are created to be. I am convinced that if we focused more on our character—rather than our career or the company we keep—we would be living more meaningful and impactful lives. We would be able to tap into the unique strengths and creative potential with which we have each been endowed. We would move beyond the cookie-cutter lives that so many have found to be shallow and unfulfilling.

As you focus this week on discovering who you truly are, your five characteristics will be linked to the topics of *Embracing, Agreeing, Capitalizing, Belonging,* and *Becoming.*

As you progress through this fast and begin to discover who God made you to be, you will be faced with the task of *Embracing* your authentic self. In order to do this, the characteristic of *Faith* will help you, keeping you rooted and grounded in authenticity.

When it comes to your value and identity, who are you *Agreeing* with? God says you are fearfully and wonderfully made. When you agree with Him, it prompts you to respond with another powerful characteristic—*Gratitude* for all He has given you.

When you understand who you really are, you can begin *Capitalizing* on your unique strengths and talents. These were given to you by God to specifically equip you for your unique *Destiny*.

Many people struggle today because they lack a sense of *Belonging*. They are lonely because they cannot be themselves around others. When you are living in your true *Identity*, the relationships you have with others will also be more authentic.

*Becoming* involves a process of growth, and the template is Jesus Christ. Jesus is the perfect example of a Man who lived with *Purpose*, and as you wrap up this week on authentic identity, your own sense of purpose should begin to be revealed to you.

# Faith

*For if we are faithful to the end, trusting God just as firmly as when we first believed, we will share in all that belongs to Christ* (Hebrews 3:14 NLT).

This week we are addressing the characteristics of an authentic person having to do with the importance of identity. Last week, we talked about the characteristics of "focus" and "order"—focusing our thoughts by ordering our day. Some days this seems to come easier than others. It's not always easy to master your time and your mind in the most effective manner. This is where faith comes in.

Believing faith will keep you rooted and grounded in authenticity. It is by faith you preserve your soul. The writer of Hebrews wrote: *"We are of those who believe and by faith preserve the soul"* (Heb. 10:39 AMP). Take charge of your day, your thoughts—and your soul—by faith.

I've grown certain that the root of all fear is that we've been forced to deny who we are. —Frances Moore Lappe

## ACTION STEPS

- Stir up your faith every moment of every day. Write down things that encourage your faith and place them where you can see them daily.

_____

_____

_____

_____

- Pinpoint those things you struggle with on a day-to-day basis that keep you from making the most of your time or distract you in the arena of your mind. How can you start removing these distractions?

_____

_____

_____

_____

_____

_____

_____

- Exercise your faith—declare what you need and confess victory over the hindrances keeping your authentic self from shining through.

_____

_____

_____

_____

_____

_____

_____

_____

*Through Him we received both the generous gift of His life and the urgent task of passing it on to others.... You are who you are through this gift and call of Jesus Christ!* (Romans 1:2)

# Gratitude

*Serve the Lord your God with joyfulness of [mind and] heart [in gratitude] for the abundance of all [with which He had blessed you]* (Deuteronomy 28:47 AMP).

Your thought life is critical to the health of your soul. And there's nothing more critical to the health of your thought life than your attitude! You've heard it said that attitude determines altitude. Today, I want to propose that it's an attitude of gratitude that determines the degree to which you will be able to live true to your authentic self.

How grateful are you for who God created you to be? Gratitude for your unique combination of strengths, abilities, and special gifts will enable you to stay true to your calling.

Look for opportunities to be grateful and to show gratitude!

*"Stay alert, with your eyes wide open in gratitude"* (Col. 4:2).

Just as you can never "out-bless" God, you can never thank Him enough either.

> The unthankful heart discovers no mercies; but let the thankful heart sweep through the day and, as the magnet finds the iron, so it will find, in every hour, some heavenly blessings! —Henry Ward Beecher

## ACTION STEPS

- What five strengths, abilities, or talents about yourself are you grateful for?

_____

_____

_____

_____

- List five opportunities or outcomes that you have not yet experienced that you can preemptively be grateful for (now you are building faith!).

_____

_____

_____

_____

_____

- Who are the people in your life you are especially grateful for? What can you do to make this known to them—and when?

_____

_____

_____

_____

_____


- How much time do you invest praising and thanking God, focusing on all the good gifts and blessings He has bestowed—versus the time you spend focusing on all that is wrong and not what you imagine it should be?

_____

_____

_____

_____

_____

*I thank Christ Jesus our Lord, who has given me strength to do His work. He considered me trustworthy and appointed me to serve Him* (1 Timothy 1:12 NLT).

# Destiny

*I'll show up and take care of you as I promised
and bring you back home. I know what I'm
doing. I have it all planned out—plans to take
care of you, not abandon you, plans to give you
the future you hope for* (Jeremiah 29:11).

Today I want to talk about destiny as it relates to living
authentically. Your divine self has a divine destiny! Over
and over in the Bible we read how God orchestrates our
destinies—how He has called and anointed all who would
*"only believe"* (Mark 5:36) to step forward and *"be strong and
courageous"* (Josh. 1:6) in taking possession of all He has
prepared for them.

To live true to your authentic self, you must continually
choose to focus on your prospective future as opposed to
your current position. Your present self is but the bud of the
full flower you are destined to become—but it's up to you to
decide whether or not you will bloom.

Your destiny is decision-oriented. If you do not like where you are, make a decision to be somewhere else. You are always only one decision away from living the life of your dreams.

> Destiny is no matter of chance. It is a matter of choice. It is not a thing to be waited for; it is a thing to be achieved. —William Jennings Bryan

## ACTION STEPS

- What do you hear God saying about who He has called you to be?

_____

_____

_____

_____

_____

- Paint a picture in your mind of your greatest possible future—write down what you see.

_____

_____

_____

_____

*You guide me with Your counsel, leading me to a glorious destiny* (Psalm 73:24 NLT).

# Identity

*In a word, what I'm saying is, "Grow up."*
*You're kingdom subjects. Now live like it. Live*
*out your God-created identity. Live generously*
*and graciously toward others, the way God lives*
*toward you* (Matthew 5:48).

As you journey toward authenticity, you must have a strong sense of identity—you must know who you are! Being confident in who God has called you to be is vital to the health of your soul and essential to your empowerment. Peter wrote, *"Once you had no identity as a people; now you are God's people"* (1 Pet. 2:10).

You carry the DNA of your Heavenly Father. Your authentic, divine self is the seed of greatness God put on the inside of you—the deposit God made when He formed *"Christ in you, the hope of glory"* (Col. 1:27 NKJV). Embrace the glory within you. God hid the potential for greatness, success, and prosperity within your identity code. Much like our genetic code, your identity code is established at the moment of conception. It provides the schematics of how you were designed to function. Crack your identity code and the contours of your life will shift and your capacity to do great things will increase.

Only by constant and continual renewal of your spirit, soul, and mind will you be able to change your beliefs about the capacity you carry for greatness. "Live out your God-created identity!"

> Your identity and your success go hand in hand. Many people sacrifice their identities by not doing what they really want to do. And that's why they're not successful. —Lila Swell

## ACTION STEPS

- What does "greatness" look like to you?

_____

_____

- If you were truly living as a king and priest, or even simply as a "new creation in Christ," how would that look? How would it feel? How would you be different?

_____

_____

_____

_____

- Get a vision for your God-created identity and write down everything you see.

_____

_____

_____

_____

_____

_____

*Those who worship Him must do it out of their very being, their spirits, their true selves* (John 4:24).

# Purpose

*Before I formed you in the womb I knew [and]
approved of you [as My chosen instrument],
and before you were born I separated and set you
apart, consecrating you* (Jeremiah 1:5 AMP).

An understanding of purpose is essential for authentic living, not only understanding your divine purpose overall, but also living purposefully—or being purpose-minded. In other words, there is living true to your calling and assignment in a general sense, but there is also being purposeful in regards to everything you do. It is a mindset as much as it is a discipline.

God created you on purpose for a purpose. It is up to you to be purposeful in understanding and firmly grasping what that purpose is. You must be intentional, deliberate, circumspect, and mindful.

It is up to you to press in to hear what God has purposed for you—and then to obey what you hear. Jesus said, *"If you refuse to do your part, you cut yourself off from God's part"* (Matt. 6:15).

> The soul which has no fixed purpose in life is lost; to be everywhere, is to be nowhere. —Michel Eyquem De Montaigne

## ACTION STEPS

- Take time today to reflect on God's purposes and how those are reflected in your own. How intentionally are you pursuing this on a daily basis?

_____

_____

_____

_____

- Write down what you hear God saying about His purpose for you in the season you are in now. Pay close attention to what God's Spirit is speaking to yours. Remember, the closer you listen, the more understanding you will be given.

_____

_____

_____

_____

- What can you be doing more of to "do your part" in bringing God's purpose for your life to pass? What should you be doing less of? Heed this advice from Proverbs: *"Form your purpose by asking for counsel, then carry it out using all the help you can get"* (Prov. 20:18).

_____

_____

_____

_____

_____

_____

*May He grant you according to your heart's desire, and fulfill all your purpose* (Psalm 20:4 NKJV).

# Week Six

## The Power of Words: Healing the Hole in Your Soul

God created words as containers to fill with our faith. Your words frame your world with great power and authority if you work in union with God. Learning to live authentically is about learning to speak truthfully about who you really are—it's about living congruently so that what you say and do align with your core values and divine nature. It's about being formed and molded—mind and mouth—into the divine blessing God created you to become. The topics that relate to this week's theme are *Eating, Legislating, Asking, Sowing,* and *Blessing.*

*Eating* refers to consuming the words of God—His Holy Scriptures. The characteristic related to this is *Integrity*—being true to your genuine essence as a unique reflection of God's glory, which happens when you have taken His words inside yourself.

*Legislating* is when you use your words to direct others and bring about God's will on Earth. This role carries a great deal of *Responsibility.*

*Asking* is how you use your words to recognize that you don't know everything and you need God's direction. When you ask, He will reveal to you areas of *Potential* that you didn't even realize existed!

Our words can plant seeds of truth in others and in ourselves—this is the power of *Sowing*. When we sow those seeds of truth in our own thinking, they will sprout into the characteristic of *Impeccability*—speaking and living the truth we have sown.

The highest use of your words is *Blessing*—setting your words free on God's behalf. The characteristic that often moves you to bless is *Compassion*, which is love in action. And love in action causes you to bless!

# Integrity

*He trained us first, passed us like silver through refining fires, brought us into hardscrabble country, pushed us to our very limit, road-tested us inside and out...finally He brought us to this well-watered place* (Psalm 66:8).

Learning to live authentically is all about learning to be true to who you really are—it's about living congruently so that what you say and do align with your core values and divine nature. It's about being formed and molded into the divine blessing God created you to be.

Living with integrity is more than "moral rectitude"— it is also being true to your genuine essence as a unique reflection of God's glory. When you are under pressure, what is revealed? Do you remain strong and immoveable when it comes to who God has called you to be?

Have you remained true to your purpose—your passions? Have you been distracted or derailed by circumstances—or have you continued to actively pursue those things that make you feel most alive?

> Try not to become a man of success but rather try to become a man of value. —Albert Einstein

## ACTION STEPS

- What are the circumstances in your life making you stronger? What is tempering you and testing your integrity?

_____

_____

_____

_____

_____

- Clarity of intent, purity of motives, honest decision-making, congruency, and transparency are all included within the concept of *integrity*. Pray and ask God to assist you in securing these virtues in your life.

_____

_____

_____

_____

_____

- As a result of this refining process, write down what you know in your heart will be revealed. What treasure are you carrying on the inside of you that needs to find expression in the world around you?

_____

_____

_____

_____

*Teach believers with your life: by word, by demeanor, by love, by faith, by integrity* (1 Timothy 4:11 MSG).

# Responsibility

*They heard the alarm but ignored it, so the
responsibility is theirs. If they had listened...they
could have saved lives* (Ezekiel 33:5).

Over the course of the past five weeks, we have talked a great
deal about your power—and essentially your obligation—to
choose and decide for yourself whether or not you will live
authentically and true to your divine nature. Do you realize
the responsibility you have to the world to become who God
is calling you to be?

It is up to you to guard your heart, govern your mindset,
harness your thoughts, discipline your behavior, and direct
your words. *You* must take responsibility.

I pray you will be among those who hear, *"Well done good
and faithful servant!"* (Matt. 25:21). Remember, no one else can
take responsibility for your life, your purpose, or your destiny
other than you.

Accept responsibility for your life. Know that it is you who will get you where you want to go, no one else.
—Les Brown

## ACTION STEPS

- What are the abilities God has given you? How well are you stewarding them?

_____

_____

_____

- Has God called you to be a leader? Of course He has! The question is: How are you taking responsibility for fulfilling that call?

_____

_____

_____

_____

- What one thing can you change that will change everything?

_____

_____

_____

_____

I want to remind us all that the world is listening, all the time. How we are ripples out from us into the world and affect others. We have a responsibility – an ability to respond – to the world. Finding our particular way of living this responsibility, of offering who we are to the world, is why we are here. We are called because the world needs us to embody the meaning in our lives. God needs us awake. The world we live in is a co-creation, a manifestation of individual consciousness woven into a collective dream. How we are with each other as individuals, as groups, as nations and tribes, is what shapes that dream. —Oriah Mountain Dreamer

*A faithful, sensible servant is one to whom the master can give the responsibility of managing* (Luke 12:42 NLT).

# Potential

*None of these things move me, neither count I my
life dear unto myself, so that I might finish my
course with joy, and the ministry, which I have
received of the Lord Jesus* (Acts 20:24 KJV).

As we journey toward authenticity, we are striving to peel
away the falsehoods, façades, and other fetters that keep us
from maximizing our true potential.

Potential is unused and unrealized power to do and to
become. And that's what this soul fast is all about—building
your capacity for the great things God has in store for you.
Refuse to be among those who never explore the hidden
potential that lies deep within—refuse to sit in front of
the television being entertained by other people's success.
When you muster up the courage to leave the shoreline of
comfort and familiarity, you can become all that you are
destined to be.

Yes, you have the potential to do all sorts of things, but you need to focus on the thing God has assigned you alone to do. Understand what your assigned "craft" is—and then master it and sail it!

> Man's main task in life is to give birth to himself, to become what he potentially is. The most important product of his effort is his own personality. —Erich Fromm

## ACTION STEPS

- What is keeping you from total expression of all that you were meant to be, to do, and to accomplish? What are the weights, doubts, fears, and other encumbrances keeping you from fully expressing your divine self?

_____

_____

_____

_____

- Ask God, "What is my assignment?"

_____

_____

_____

_____

- Ask yourself, "What have I invested in maximizing my potential in that area?"

_____

_____

_____

_____

- Envision what your potential maximized would look like. Now, imagine how it might look with God working in and through you! Ask God to show you, and then ask Him to do it!

_____

_____

_____

_____

*No eye has seen, no ear has heard, and no mind has imagined what God has prepared for those who love Him* (1 Corinthians 2:9 NLT).

# Impeccability

*Don't say anything you don't mean...You only
make things worse when you lay down a smoke
screen of pious talk, saying, "I'll pray for you,"
and never doing it, or saying, "God be with you,"
and not meaning it. You don't make your words
true by embellishing them with religious lace.
In making your speech sound more religious, it
becomes less true. Just say "yes" and "no." When
you manipulate words to get your own way, you
go wrong* (Matthew 5:33).

Impeccability. I love this word. I love this characteristic.
Impeccability is what kept satan from having any power
over Jesus (see John 14:30 NLT). Where sin leads to defeat
and death, impeccability leads to victory and increasingly
abundant life.

So how do we adopt this characteristic into our everyday
lives? I think of John 1:47 where Jesus said of Nathanael,

*"Here is an Israelite indeed…in whom there is no guile"* (John 1:47 AMP). Or, as other translations say, *"no deceit"* (NKJV), *"nothing false"* (NCV), and *"a man of complete integrity"* (NLT). In other words, a man who is honest, transparent, has nothing to hide, who is living life inside out, a man who is living authentically, *"free of error, mixed motives, or hidden agendas"* (1 Thess. 2:3).

Authenticity has to do with honesty—do you always speak the truth? Do you say one thing when you mean another or misrepresent what you are truly feeling or thinking? The Bible speaks of one thing alone that makes a person perfect, and that is perfectly true words. James wrote, *"If anyone does not stumble in word, he is a perfect man"* (James 3:2 NKJV).

> Be impeccable with your word. Speak with integrity. Say only what you mean. Avoid using the word to speak against yourself or to gossip about others. Use the power of your word in the direction of truth and love. —Miguel Angel Ruiz

## ACTION STEPS

- Do you always speak the truth? Do you say one thing when you mean another or misrepresent what you are truly feeling or thinking?

_____

_____

_____

_____

- How have you used words against yourself?

_____

_____

_____

_____

- How "free of error, mixed motives, or hidden agendas" are you living? How transparent is your life and speech?

_____

_____

_____

_____

- Would Jesus say of you, "Look, there goes a person in whom there is no guile"?

_____

_____

_____

_____

*If you could find someone whose speech was perfectly true, you'd have a perfect person, in perfect control of life* (James 3:2 MSG).

# Compassion

*It's quite simple…be compassionate and loyal in your love, and don't take yourself too seriously* (Micah 6:8).

In the last few days, we've talked about *responsibility, potential,* and *impeccability.* Today, I want to talk to you about *compassion*—because without this characteristic, you will have a difficult time fully walking in any of the other characteristics of an authentic person. American Author, Frederick Buechner said, "Compassion is sometimes the fatal capacity for feeling what it is like to live inside somebody else's skin. It is the knowledge that there can never really be any peace and joy for me until there is peace and joy finally for you too."

I encourage you today to check your compassion meter. Open your heart and mind to those in need around you and explore how you might respond to those needs. Speak a blessing into the lives of everyone you encounter.

What better way is there to share the love of God than to bless others with your words? That is how you shine light into dark places!

Too often we underestimate the power of a touch, a smile, a kind word, a listening ear, an honest accomplishment, or the smallest act of caring, all of which have the potential to turn a life around. —Leo Buscaglia

## ACTION STEPS

- Think of someone you normally don't have patience for, and speak a blessing over him or her now.

_____

_____

_____

_____

- The next time you come across a person less fortunate, stop and bless them with your words. You might not have the money or time to invest, but you always have a kind word— and there is no better investment than that.

_____

_____

_____

_____

## Compassion

*So be merciful (sympathetic, tender, responsive, and compassionate) even as your Father is* (Luke 6:36 AMP).

# Week Seven

## The Power of Doing: God's Chosen Fast

The debate over whether people should focus on who they are or what they do is as ancient as the Torah itself. God created both, and they cannot be easily separated. In a previous week you looked at who you are regarding your identity apart from what you do—this week you will focus on the *do* part of you. The focus topics of *doing* are *Helping, Partnering, Continuing, Prioritizing,* and *Willing.*

*Helping* will require you to believe the best of people. Believing in people will lead you into this day's characteristic— showing *Respect* for others.

Your chances of thriving in life are considerably higher if you are *Partnering* with someone else who is also thriving. When you have locked arms with such quality people, make sure to place a high value on *Loyalty*—keep them around!

As you are *Continuing* through this soul fast, you are always one decision away from changing the course of your life and from living the life of your dreams. Your choices and behaviors establish your *Credibility*.

The highest priority on your list must always be staying connected to the Presence of God and listening to His still, small voice. *Prioritizing* God-things above selfish desires will help you live a life characterized by *Temperance*.

Finally, be *Willing* to run headlong into your destiny. Learning to harness the power of holiness by doing things God's way—by developing strong *Morality*—will bring you true success and freedom.

# Respect

*Make the Master proud of you by being good citizens. Respect the authorities, whatever their level; they are God's emissaries for keeping order. It is God's will that by doing good, you might cure the ignorance of the fools who think you're a danger to society. Exercise your freedom by serving God, not by breaking the rules. Treat everyone you meet with dignity. Love your spiritual family. Revere God. Respect the government* (1 Peter 2:13-17).

Akin to showing compassion is showing respect. Without the ability to respect the rights, opinions, and differences of others, you won't be able to show compassion toward those who might not think or look or behave like you.

If you want to be respected, you must show respect. This is why humility comes before honor. Those who are unable to honor and respect all people will themselves never become honorable.

The Bible tells us to *"show respect for all people"* (1 Pet. 2:17 NCV) and *"show respect and honor to them all"* (Rom. 13:7 NCV). You cannot "demand" respect, but only "command" it by taking action on behalf of others.

> There is no better way to thank God for your sight than by giving a *helping* hand to someone in the dark. —Helen Keller

> Do what you can, with what you have, where you are. —Theodore Roosevelt

## ACTION STEPS

- What one thing can you do today to honor someone?

_____

_____

_____

- To what degree do you command respect? Are you a leader others look up to because you are respectful—as in "full of respect?"

_____

_____

_____

_____

_____

_____

*He rekindles burned-out lives with fresh hope, restoring dignity and respect to their lives—a place in the sun* (1 Samuel 2:6 MSG).

# Loyalty

*Don't lose your grip on Love and Loyalty. Tie them around your neck; carve their initials on your heart. Earn a reputation for living well in God's eyes and the eyes of the people* (Proverbs 3:3).

Last week we focused on the power of our words, highlighting the authentic characteristics of impeccability, compassion, and respect—demonstrating that our words are simply a reflection of what is in our hearts. Beyond words is how we choose to behave—what we choose to do and the decisions we make every moment of every day.

If you want to lock arms and do life with quality people of understanding who are trustworthy and loyal, you will have to prove yourself loyal.

The degree to which you show yourself loyal to God— faithful, obedient, being true to your word, making good on your obligations and promises, and God-fearing—will determine to what extent you are able to live authentically.

Loyalty is the pledge of truth to oneself and others.
—Ada Velez-Boardley

## ACTION STEPS

- How is God's loyalty working in *and* through your life?

_____

_____

_____

_____

_____

- In what areas might your loyalties be "divided"? What can you do to change that?

_____

_____

_____

_____

_____

- How has someone's disloyalty affected you in the past? Sometimes reflecting on that will compel you be more loyal.

_____

_____

_____

_____

*Do not waver, for a person with divided loyalty is as unsettled as a wave of the sea that is blown and tossed by the wind.... Their loyalty is divided between God and the world, and they are unstable in everything they do* (James 1:6, 8 NLT).

# Credibility

*Remove impurities from the silver and the silversmith can craft a fine chalice; remove the wicked from leadership and authority will be credible and God honoring* (Proverbs 25:4).

This week we are focusing on the power of doing. What we do is a result of the decisions we make and the actions we take as a result. You are always one decision away from changing the course of your life and from living the life of your dreams. Your choices and behaviors establish your credibility.

*Credibility* simply means "believability." Are you someone who says one thing and does another? Can people believe what you say? Without establishing your credibility—your believability—you will never be true to yourself. There is no deception worse than self-deception! You must hold yourself accountable for your own legitimacy, genuineness, and yes, authenticity. This is what lasting reputations are built upon.

Ultimately, *you* are the product. *You* are the dream, the service, the idea, the message, even the Gospel made flesh.

The more you are willing to accept responsibility for your actions, the more credibility you will have. — Brian Koslow

## ACTION STEPS

- Consciously strive to create credibility. Practice proven credibility boosters such as being honest, being on time, being a person of your word—being dependable.

_____

_____

_____

- What is your promise to the world? Establishing credibility is only a means to an end, not the end itself. What can people count on you to do because you are here? What do you stand for? How will you leave your mark?

_____

_____

_____

_____

_____

*He honoureth those who fear the Lord, those who revere the Lord. He who sweareth an oath, or who promiseth, to his neighbour, and deceiveth him not. (Psalm 15:4 WYC)*

Day
Thirty-four

# Temperance

*Yes, in the past you lived the way the world lives, following the ruler of the evil powers that are above the earth. That same spirit is now working in those who refuse to obey God. In the past all of us lived like them, trying to please our sinful selves and doing all the things our bodies and minds wanted* (Ephesians 2:2-3 NCV).

You don't hear much about the characteristic of "temperance" these days. Temperance is sort of an old-fashioned word that is defined as "moderation in action, thought, or feeling: restraint—habitual moderation in the indulgence of the appetites or passions."

We have actually spoken a great deal about taming the appetites as a central purpose for this *40-Day Soul Fast*— making *"no provision for [indulging] the flesh"* (Rom. 13:14 AMP) and abstaining *"from fleshly lusts, which war against the soul"* (1 Pet. 2:11 KJV).

Temperance is one of the seven attributes we are told to *"add to our faith"* by Peter (see 2 Peter 1:1-7) and one of the nine fruits of the Spirit Paul wrote to the Galatians about. (See Gal. 5:22-23.)

Great leaders have fallen because of their lack of self-control. Accomplished men and women of God have compromised their faith and ministry simply because they were unable to exercise restraint.

Don't use your lack of moderation or self-restraint in some area to keep you from your better self.

> Being forced to work, and forced to do your best, will breed in you temperance and self-control, diligence and strength of will, cheerfulness and contentment, and a hundred virtues which the idle will never know.
> —Charles Kingsley

## ACTION STEPS

- Examine your life. Where might the enemy have a foothold in the door of your soul, causing you to stumble in some area?

_____

_____

_____

_____

_____

- What can you do to "clean house" in order to make sure you are *"temperate in all things?"* What might your little "excesses" say to others about you?

_____

_____

_____

_____

_____

_____

*Moderation is better than muscle, self-control better than political power* (Proverbs 16:32).

# Morality

*It is obvious what kind of life develops out of trying to get your own way all the time...a stinking accumulation of mental and emotional garbage; frenzied and joyless grabs for happiness...paranoid loneliness; cutthroat competition; all-consuming-yet-never-satisfied wants; a brutal temper; an impotence to love or be loved; divided homes and divided lives; small-minded and lopsided pursuits; the vicious habit of depersonalizing everyone into a rival; uncontrolled and uncontrollable addictions* (Galatians 5:19-21).

This week we are talking about what I call "the power of doing." What you *do* can be as toxic to your soul as what you *think* or *say*—your actions have as much power to pollute or purify as your thoughts and words.

Morality simply means virtuous conduct—"behavior or qualities judged to be good"—based on a set of principles distinguishing between right and wrong or good and bad behavior. It's doing things God's way. It is drawing the line in the sand and saying this far and no further. Morality is a serious thing. Barry McGuire said, "And there was a real shedding of the old dogma, like boundaries of morality were being broken down and everybody was into the new party mode...which destroyed thousands of us."

In this success-driven society, it is odd to think that the bottom line might not be what we expect it is—success might not look like we think it does. At the end of the day, morality boils down to a life and death issue. We cannot afford to sit on the wall of indifference and expect society to change all by itself. As with beautiful art, the lines of morality must be deliberately drawn.

> I never did, or countenanced, in public life, a single act inconsistent with the strictest good faith; having never believed there was one code of morality for a public, and another for a private man. —Thomas Jefferson

## ACTION STEPS

- Are you having difficulty "directing your energies wisely"? Check to make sure you're doing whatever you do "God's way" and not your own way.

_____

_____

_____

- Stop and reflect for a few moments on the verse at the beginning of this day's reading. Are any of the indicators listed here of "what happens when you do things your own way" present in your life?

_____

_____

_____

_____

*We find ourselves involved in loyal commitments, not needing to force our way in life, able to marshal and direct our energies wisely"* (Galatians 5:22-23).

# Week Eight

## Sealing the Healing: The Cleansing Power of Love

In this final week of *The 40 Day Soul Fast*, we are talking about the power of love at work in our lives. Truly authentic people reach a place where the love of God is activated in their lives and in their dealings with others. Love is the capstone on this eight-week journey—the greatest expression of the most authentic you.

As we look at the power of love, we address themes of *Dancing, Accepting, Standing, Uniting,* and *Telling.*

*Dancing* means living life together with God—doing His work as a partner with Him and loving people in your actions. The characteristic of *Justice* will emerge when you're living together with God this way.

Authentic people have come to a place of *Accepting* those who are commonly marginalized. It's another way you can live out God's love for them. The world understands this attribute by the name of *Tolerance*, which is more than just "putting up with" differences. It gives you the capacity to be merciful.

Being and doing come down to this—*Standing*. Taking your place, your God-given destiny, and refusing to be moved. The characteristic is *Ethics*, because ethics are your guidelines and an excellent place to root yourself.

Breaking down barriers between people and drawing us closer together—that's *Uniting*. Uniting is living in community—in love. The characteristic of *Interdependence* means something similar—we are not ourselves alone; we need each other to live authentic lives!

The final step is *Telling* others—sharing our testimony with the world. This brings us into a close-knit *Community* of people who do life together, share their stories, and live in harmony with God, each other, and their authentic selves!

# Justice

*For unto us a Child is born, unto us a Son is given; and the government will be upon His shoulder. And His name will be called Wonderful, Counselor, Mighty God, Everlasting Father, Prince of Peace. Of the increase of His government and peace there will be no end, upon the throne of David and over His kingdom, to order it and establish it with judgment and justice from that time forward, even forever. The zeal of the Lord of hosts will perform this* (Isaiah 9:6-7).

Yesterday we talked about the characteristic of morality and why it is so important in your journey toward authenticity. Justice, like morality, has to do with our actions and behaviors. Justice, however, takes us one step further in that it has more to do with how we treat other people than it does following a set of principles regarding how we conduct our personal lives. Justice is about what we do on behalf of others.

A person who has a sense of justice treats others with fairness, is respectful of the rights and needs of others, and is non-partial when it comes to showing kindness and mercy. This person will feel compelled to intercede on behalf of those less fortunate or speak up on behalf of someone who is being treated unfairly.

Without justice and love, peace will always be the great illusion. —Archbishop Helder Pessoa Camara

## ACTION STEPS

- How might you be neglecting the weightier matters of justice and mercy?

_____

_____

_____

- What can you begin doing today to "serve people" and make sure evil does not thrive unopposed?

_____

_____

_____

_____

_____

*The Lord has told you, human, what is good; He has told you what He wants from you: to do what is right to other people, love being kind to others, and live humbly, obeying your God* (Micah 6:8 NCV).

# Tolerance

*Through His faithfulness, God displayed Jesus as the place of sacrifice where mercy is found by means of His blood. He did this to demonstrate His righteousness in passing over sins that happened before, during the time of God's patient tolerance. He also did this to demonstrate that He is righteous in the present time, and to treat the one who has faith in Jesus as righteous* (Romans 3:25-26 CEB).

God is much bigger than your view of Him, and He will use all kinds of people—especially those on the margins—to broaden your understanding of that. Your task is to love and accept them where they are. Human beings will never be able to fully "map" out God, but it will take the experiences of each one to even get a small glimpse.

Tolerance is the ability to accept the differences of others. It enables you to show patience, compassion, and charity.

Tolerance can also be defined as "the power or capacity of an organism to tolerate unfavorable environmental conditions." Imagine what that kind of power could do for you.

When you exercise tolerance, you are exercising your faith in the power of God's goodness to soften hearts and His grace to overpower evil.

> When you find peace within yourself, you become the kind of person who can live at peace with others.
> —Mildred Lisette Norman

## ACTION STEPS

- How would you rate your capacity to tolerate unfavorable conditions? What does this say about your own degree of personal empowerment?

_____

_____

_____

_____

- How are you harnessing the power of tolerance to change the hearts and lives of those around you? In what small way might you show a little more tolerance?

_____

_____

_____

*He who is slow to anger has great understanding, but he who is hasty of spirit exposes and exalts his folly* (Proverbs 14:29 AMP).

# Ethics

*When you're kind to others, you help yourself;
when you're cruel to others, you hurt yourself.
Bad work gets paid with a bad check; good work
gets solid pay. Take your stand with God's loyal
community and live, or chase after phantoms of
evil and die. God can't stand deceivers, but oh
how He relishes integrity* (Proverbs 11:17-20).

As we wind down our *40 Day Soul Fast*, we are talking
about the importance of "being" and "doing"—the impact
our behaviors and actions have on the world around us—
and how that in turn is reflected back to us in the way we
experience life.

We began this journey toward authenticity talking about
the inner life of the soul. As we have progressed through the
40 days, we have moved out from our own internal awareness
of the life of our soul to an understanding of the power of
our thoughts, our identity, and our words. This week, we are

talking about how all of these elements affect how we relate to others.

Becoming more authentic, more genuine, more "real" requires a deeper sense of truthfulness, honesty, and honor. Our truest intentions are revealed. Our integrity is tested. Our credibility is established. This is what the concept of *ethics* represents: That which is motivated by pure, noble, and honorable intentions—an uprightness in choices, values, business dealings, and professional aspirations. Your sense of ethics will require you to take a stand.

Those whose hearts are upright before God will be required to stand up on behalf of those can't stand up for themselves—to stand up for the oppressed—to stand up against evil! Let your life make a statement by taking a stand.

> The ultimate measure of a man is not where he stands in moments of comfort and convenience, but where he stands at times of challenge and controversy.
> —Martin Luther King Jr.

## ACTION STEPS

- In bringing something to your attention, could God be requiring you to take a stand?

_____

_____

_____

_____

_____

- Write down some thoughts about the quote: "You are only as powerful as that for which you stand."

_____

_____

_____

_____

- "Unless we stand for something, we shall fall for anything." How do you see this truth working in your own life?

_____

_____

_____

_____

*If you don't take your stand in faith, you won't have a leg to stand on* (Isaiah 7:7).

# Interdependence

*You can easily enough see how this kind of thing
works by looking no further than your own body.
Your body has many parts—limbs, organs,
cells—but no matter how many parts you can
name, you're still one body. It's exactly the same
with Christ. By means of His one Spirit, we
all said good-bye to our partial and piecemeal
lives. We each used to independently call our
own shots, but then we entered into a large and
integrated life in which He has the final say in
everything* (1 Corinthians 12:12).

Whether you love people by giving financially, by sharing
your wisdom and knowledge, or by exercising your gifts
and talents, your life is directly united to others and is
interdependent on their reciprocating acts of love toward
you. Mark Twain once said: "To get the full value of joy you

must have someone to divide it with." Love others lavishly—because in truth, you are showering love on yourself!

Yesterday we talked about ethics and taking a stand on behalf of others—today we will focus on why this is so important. Interestingly, the more authentic we become, the more interdependent we will be. As the dividing walls and facades come down, we learn to trust in and rely on one another—we realize we need each other to complete one another.

> I can never be what I ought to be until you are what you ought to be. This is the way our world is made. No individual or nation can stand out boasting of being independent. We are interdependent. — Martin Luther King, Jr.

## ACTION STEPS

- How deep is your sense of interdependence?

_____

_____

_____

- Where do you fit in to bring more completion to the Body of Christ?

_____

_____

_____

_____

- What dividing walls are you still putting up to keep yourself independent? What can you do to start taking them down today, one brick at a time?

_____

_____

_____

_____

*In the same way, we are many, but in Christ we are all one body. Each one is a part of that body, and each part belongs to all the other parts* (Romans 12:5 NCV).

# Community

*Above all things have intense and unfailing love for one another, for love covers a multitude of sins [forgives and disregards the offenses of others]* (1 Peter 4:8 AMP).

Connection, collaboration, communication, acceptance, compassion, respect, support, safety, shared values, inclusion, kindness, tolerance, understanding, and inspiration are a few words that come to mind when I think of community. Our communities need to be healed, and we can start by healing our own souls so that we can walk in authentic love.

As we bring our journey to a close, I want to talk to you about what I believe is the nearest and dearest thing to God's heart: Building authentic community.

Building community is not a political or economic process, but purely spiritual and relational. It is ultimately about corporate destiny—our destiny as a collaborative entity. It is about living and working together so that we can make this world a better place for everyone.

When you build community, there is no big "I" and little "you," but simply "we" and "us."

This is what living in community is all about. It's God's best will for His people. It's what floods the world with light and turns it upside right.

> And as we let our own light shine, we unconsciously give other people permission to do the same. As we are liberated from our own fear, our presence automatically liberates others.—Marianne Williamson

## ACTION STEPS

- From this day forward, how will you shine a little brighter? Describe what that might look like and the affect it could have on the people you encounter.

_____

_____

_____

_____

_____

_____

_____

_____

- Change begins one thought, one soul, one life at a time. What is the one thought you can adopt that could change everything? What will be the new story you tell as a result?

_____

_____

_____

_____

- How can you start a conversation in your community—whether it is the workplace, church, neighborhood, or school—about living more authentically?

_____

_____

_____

_____

_____

*Your love for one another will prove to the world that you are My disciples"* (John 13:35 NLT).

*We can't help but thank God for you, because your faith is flourishing and your love for one another is growing* (2 Thessalonians 1:3 NLT).

# Ask yourself these 24 questions:

1.  Who am I outside of the roles I play?

2.  What are my long-term goals?

3.  What should I be doing with my life right now?

4.  What are my strengths?

5.  What are my weaknesses?

6.  What direction will my life go if I continue doing what I'm doing?

7.  How can I be sure I am in the right place, doing the right thing?

8.  What is my purpose?

9.  Who should I be partnering with?

10. What resources are available for me to accomplish my goals?

11. Do I like the person I've become?

12. What do I really want to achieve in this lifetime?

13. What brings me my greatest joy?

14. What am I really passionate about?

15. What frustrates me most or makes me sad?

16. If I could do something other than what I am doing now, what would that be?

17. If I could live somewhere else, where would that be?

18. Do these things that I do and am involved with make me feel good and happy?

19. Are my relationships mutually beneficial and symbiotic?

20. Is there room for improvement in my relationships?

21. What have I accomplished so far with my life? Is it enough?

22. If I could do one thing different, what would it be?

23. After my death, will future generations know that I lived?

24. How do I want people to remember me?

# Empowering You for Life!

## LOOKING FOR MORE?

Please visit me online at www.trimminternational.com for more tools and resources to nurture the life of your soul. If you want to take part in the Soul Fast Movement, please go to www.soulfast.com to find out how you can get involved, enroll in our ongoing programs, or participate in a guided, interactive 40 Day Soul Fast. Two times per year, I host an eight-week program when I personally coach you through each of the 40 Characteristics via my weekly empowerment broadcast, daily video blog, and downloadable phone app. There you also will find a *40 Day Soul Fast Cleansing Guide*, a free "Dynamic Life Questionnaire," an online community where you can always continue the conversation, as well as other soul-enhancing resources.

Let's do life together! Join with me as I endeavor to heal the world by healing the souls of individuals—empowering them to impact their communities and nations all across the globe. Every soul is significant and influences the world in countless ways. Never doubt that what you do *does* make a difference! You could be the answer someone else is looking for. Don't wait another day to step up to the plate—the world's next homerun could be depending on you to make the pitch. Pitch life. Pitch healing!

I value you and what you bring to the game. Let's make a difference and bring healing wherever we are. Let's make this life a winning proposition for all. For more about soul healing and empowerment, please visit me online. Join the soul healing movement or create your own. If you are interested in pioneering the unexplored frontiers of your own destiny, enroll in my signature *Executive Life Coaching* personal and professional achievement program, or join my *Life Empowerment Program*, offering practical insights to help you maximize your potential every single day of the year.

As always, I look forward to empowering you for life!

Dr. Cindy Trimm

# More Empowerment Initiatives From

## Dr. Cindy Trimm

Imagine The Possibilities!

Executive Life Coaching with Dr. Cindy Trimm is a 52-week success system for maximum personal and professional achievement. Join an elite group of protégés as Dr. Trimm takes you on an epic destiny-fulfilling journey.

From spearheading health outreaches in the inner city to building homes for orphans in southeast Asia, the Trimm Foundation strives to bring practical solutions and empowerment strategies to the places where hope and healing are needed most.

The Life Empowerment Program provides you with 365-days of life strategies designed to unlock your fullest potential. As your empowerment mentor, each day Dr. Cindy Trimm will share key principles and insights that will take you where you want to be a year from today. Imagine where your life could be this time next year! By making just a few adjustments, taking deliberate action with a little focused effort and conscious intention, you will make quantum progress. This is what this program is all about.

Receive a daily e-video teaching packed with practical life principles that will equip you to:

- Grow emotionally, professionally, relationally

- Discover and unlock the seed of greatness hidden with you

- Dramatically increase your ability to fulfill any goal or desire

- Add meaning to what you're doing

- Expand your influence with others

- Learn what it takes to win at life

- Put the "wow" back into daily living

Sign up today at www.yourlifeempowerment.com or call us at 866-444-7258.

Dr. Trimm is looking to heal communities by empowering individuals. Keep your eyes open for Dr. Trimm's upcoming book and worldwide campaign:

*Heal Your Soul, Heal Our World.*

Together, we can heal the world!

Visit www.TrimmInternational.com today!

## SOON TO BE RELEASED:

*Heal Your Soul, Heal Our World*

*Reclaim Your Soul*

*Reclaim Your Health*

*The Creed*

*The Quest*

*The Journey*

# OTHER RESOURCES FOR SPIRITUAL ENRICHMENT FROM DR. TRIMM INCLUDE:

*The Prayer Warrior's Way*

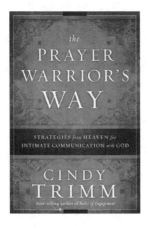

*The Art of War for Spiritual Battle*

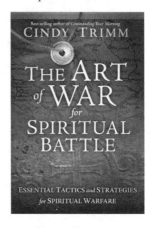

*Commanding Your Morning*

*The Rules of Engagement*

## Discover Your AQ

What's Your Authenticity Quotient?
Be sure to visit www.soulfast.com to take the
free AQ Assessment and find out how authentically
you are living today!

## Get the App

Share with your friends.
Track your progress
Keep up with your journal.
Change your life.
The 40 Day Soul Fast App

http://soulfast.destinyimage.com

# About Dr. Cindy Trimm

A best-selling author, high impact teacher, and former senator, Dr. Trimm is a sought-after empowerment specialist, revolutionary thinker, and transformational leader. She has earned a distinguished reputation as a catalyst for change and voice of hope to the nations.

Listed among *Ebony* magazine's *Power 100* as the "top 100 doers and influencers in the world today," Dr. Trimm is a featured speaker on some of the world's largest platforms, a frequent guest on Christian broadcasting's most popular TV and radio shows, and continually tops the Black Christian News Network and Black Christian Book Company's National Bestsellers List.

Dr. Trimm combines her wealth of leadership expertise with her depth of spiritual understanding to reveal life-transforming messages that empower and inspire. Seasoned with humor, compassion, revelatory insight, and personal candor, Dr. Trimm opens minds and touches hearts with biblically-based principles of inner healing and personal empowerment.

Pulling on her background in government, education, psychology, and human development, Dr. Trimm translates hard-hitting spiritual insights into everyday language that empower individuals to transform their lives—helping change the path people take in search of meaning, dignity, purpose, and hope.

# Notes

# Notes

*Notes*

# In the right hands, This Book will Change Lives!

Most of the people who need this message will not be looking for this book. To change their lives, you need to put a copy of this book in their hands.

> But others (seeds) fell into good ground, and brought forth fruit, some a hundred-fold, some sixty-fold, some thirty-fold (Matthew 13:8).

Our ministry is constantly seeking methods to find the good ground, the people who need this anointed message to change their lives. Will you help us reach these people?

> Remember this—a farmer who plants only a few seeds will get a small crop. But the one who plants generously will get a generous crop (2 Corinthians 9:6).

## EXTEND THIS MINISTRY BY SOWING
### 3 BOOKS, 5 BOOKS, 10 BOOKS, OR MORE TODAY,
#### AND BECOME A LIFE CHANGER!

Thank you,

Don Nori Sr., Founder
Destiny Image
Since 1982

## DESTINY IMAGE PUBLISHERS, INC.

*"Promoting Inspired Lives."*

### VISIT OUR NEW SITE HOME AT
### WWW.DESTINYIMAGE.COM

---

### FREE SUBSCRIPTION TO DI NEWSLETTER

Receive free unpublished articles by top DI authors, exclusive
discounts, and free downloads from our best and newest books.

**Visit www.destinyimage.com to subscribe.**

---

Write to:     Destiny Image
              P.O. Box 310
              Shippensburg, PA 17257-0310

Call:     1-800-722-6774

Email:     orders@destinyimage.com

For a complete list of our titles or to place an order
online, visit www.destinyimage.com.